Ancient Myths

The Voyages of Odysseus

Written by
Sue Reid

Illustrated by
Mark Bergin

Created and designed by
David Salariya

PiCTURE WiNDOW BOOKS
Minneapolis, Minnesota

First published in the United States in 2005
by Picture Window Books
5115 Excelsior Boulevard
Minneapolis, MN 55416
1-877-845-8392
www.picturewindowbooks.com

First published in Great Britain in 2004 by Book House,
an imprint of The Salariya Book Company, Ltd.,
25 Marlborough Place, Brighton BN1 1UB
Please visit The Salariya Book Company at
www.salariya.com or *www.book-house.co.uk*

Library of Congress Cataloging-in-Publication Data
Reid, Sue (Susan)
The voyages of Odysseus / by Sue Reid ; illustrated by Mark
Bergin.
    p. cm.—(Ancient myths)
Includes index.
ISBN 1-4048-0905-8 (hardcover)
1. Mythology, Greek—Juvenile literature. I. Bergin, Mark. II.
Title. III. Series.
BL820.03R45 2004
398.2'0938'02–dc22   2004007369

Content Adviser: Professor William D. Dyer, Humanities Director,
English Department, Minnesota State University, Mankato

Editors: Michael Ford, Nadia Higgins

About the Author: Sue Reid began writing stories when she
was a child and now writes for BBC Schools Radio. Her first
book, *Mill Girl,* was published by Scholastic in 2002.
She would like to dedicate *The Voyages of Odysseus*
to William, Matt, and Guy.

About the Illustrator: Mark Bergin studied at Eastbourne
College of Art and has illustrated many children's books. He lives
in Bexhill-on-Sea, England, with his wife and three children.

About the Series Creator: David Salariya was born in Dundee,
Scotland. He has illustrated a wide range of books and has
created and designed many new series for publishers worldwide.
In 1989, he established The Salariya Book Company. He lives in
Brighton, England, with his wife, illustrator Shirley Willis, and
their son Jonathan.

For more information on *Odysseus,* use FactHound
to track down Web sites related to this book.

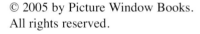

  1. Go to *www.facthound.com*
  2. Type in this book ID: 1404809058
  3. Click on the *Fetch It* button.

Your trusty FactHound will fetch the best Web sites for you!

Printed and bound in China.
Printed on paper from sustainable forests.

The Voyages of Odysseus

Table of Contents

The World of Ancient Mythology

The ancient Greek civilization was one of the greatest in the history of the world. It spanned nearly 2,000 years, until it was eventually overtaken by the Roman Empire in the second century B.C. At its height, the ancient Greek world extended far beyond what we know as modern Greece.

We owe much to the ancient Greeks. They were great scientists, mathematicians, dramatists, and philosophers. They were also brilliant storytellers. Many of the tales they told were in the form of poetry, often thousands of lines long. The Greeks wrote poems about all kinds of human experiences—love, friendship, war, revenge, history, and even simple everyday activities. The most famous of the poems that have passed down to us are the epic tales of courage and warfare, where brave heroes struggle and suffer against great odds.

A map showing the ancient Greek mainland, surrounding islands, and territories

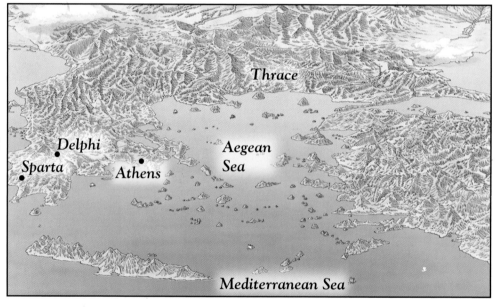

It is incredible that until the eighth century B.C., the Greeks had no established form of writing. All of their stories, lengthy as they were, were handed down through every generation by word of mouth. The people who passed on these tales were professional storytellers. They would perform in town squares or public theaters. Often, several versions of the same myth existed, depending on who told it and when it was told. What follows is one version of the voyages of Odysseus.

If you need help with any of the names, go to the pronunciation guide on page 31.

4

Introduction

Gather round and hear my story. I shall tell you about one of the greatest heroes Greece has ever known—the brave Odysseus, king of the island of Ithaca. His story began when he joined his Greek comrades to fight the city of Troy. For 10 years, they besieged the city until Odysseus—the most cunning of the Greeks—found a way to trick the Trojans and end the war. He and some warriors hid inside a huge wooden horse, hoping the Trojans would drag it into the city. Foolishly, this is just what the Trojans did! At night, the Greeks climbed out and opened the city gates for their comrades. Surprised by their enemies, the Trojans were defeated. Sick of war and eager to be reunited with his wife, Penelope, Odysseus and his fleet of 12 ships were at last able to go home.

5

From One Feast to the Next

Traveling back to Ithaca, Odysseus and his men first landed at Ismarus, a city in Thrace. They rampaged through the city, looting and killing, before hurrying back to their boats. Odysseus wisely wanted to leave before the locals could seek revenge, but his men chose to feast. They fell into a drunken sleep, only to be awakened by the shouts of the Cicones, neighboring warriors who had come to avenge the deaths of their friends. There was bloody fighting, and though the Greeks escaped to their ships, 72 of their men were killed.

Grieving for their dead comrades, the men sailed onward to the land of the Lotus-Eaters. There, Odysseus sent three of his men to scope out the land. When they didn't return, he went in search of them. At last, Odysseus found the men wandering around in a daze and dragged them back to their ships.

The raid on Ismarus

The Greeks plundered the city of Ismarus, stealing treasure and supplies of water, food, and wine for their voyage home.

Ask the storyteller

What made Odysseus's men so dazed?

The Lotus-Eaters had given the men the fruit of the lotus plant to eat. The fruit made the men forget all about who they were and where they were headed.

Polyphemus the Cyclops

Sailing on, the men reached the land of the cyclopes. Odysseus was eager to find out what these one-eyed giants were like. He led a party of men into one of their caves. Soon its owner returned—the gigantic Polyphemus—with one eye staring out from the middle of his forehead. Polyphemus was very angry to find the men in his home. He immediately seized and ate two of them for his supper. Then he made sure the others couldn't escape by blocking the cave's entrance with a huge boulder. The men were terrified, but the wily Odysseus soon figured out a way to escape. The following night, while Polyphemus was asleep, the men sharpened a wooden stake and blinded the cyclops with it. In the morning, when Polyphemus rolled away the boulder to let his sheep out, the men sneaked out as well. The enraged cyclops called on the god Poseidon for revenge.

Odysseus tricks the cyclops

In the morning, the blinded Polyphemus sat in the cave entrance and felt each sheep's back to make sure the men didn't try to ride the sheep out. He didn't find the men though, because they were tied under the sheep's bellies.

9

Ask the storyteller

Why did Polyphemus ask Poseidon for help?

Polyphemus was one of Poseidon's sons. To avenge his son's blindness, Poseidon vowed to stop Odysseus from ever returning home.

Keeper of the Winds

Next, Odysseus and his men reached the island ruled by King Aeolus, the god of the winds. Aeolus welcomed Odysseus and gave him a mysterious leather bag, which he told him never to open. Then the king sent a gentle breeze after the ships to guide them home. However, when Odysseus's back was turned, his greedy crew opened the bag, looking for treasure. Out rushed terrible storms, which drove the ships back to the island. This time Aeolus refused to help the men. Worse was to come. Setting out again, they were blown to the land of the Laestrygonians. There, the unfortunate crew met King Antiphates, a man-eating giant, who promptly gobbled up one of Odysseus's men. The rest of the men fled back to their ships, chased by the giants.

The Laestrygonians

The angry Laestrygonians pursued Odysseus's men as they fled back to their ships. The giants hurled boulders and spears at the crew as they tried to escape. Trapped in the harbor, all the ships were sunk except Odysseus's.

How did Odysseus manage to escape?

Odysseus had wisely anchored his ship outside the harbor. By doing so, he was able to quickly sail out of danger.

Circe the Enchantress

Mourning their dead friends, Odysseus and his crew sailed on to Circe's island. Circe was a wicked sorceress, who used her magic to turn men into beasts. All around her house were tame lions and wolves—men who'd been bewitched by her. Nevertheless, the crew landed, and some of the men went to Circe's house to seek help. Circe made Odysseus's men very welcome, but after they'd eaten her delicious food, she struck them with her wand and turned them into pigs. Only one man, Eurylochus, escaped, because he'd wisely stayed outside. When he saw what had happened to his comrades, he rushed back to the ship to warn Odysseus. Odysseus set off at once to confront Circe. On his way, he met Hermes, messenger of the gods, who showed the hero how to protect himself against Circe's magic.

Odysseus confronts Circe

When Circe struck Odysseus with her wand, he quickly drew his sword. Fearful that Odysseus meant to kill her, Circe immediately agreed to turn his men back into humans.

Ask the storyteller

How did Hermes protect Odysseus?

Circe secretly mixed a magic potion into the men's food to make them forget where they came from. Hermes gave Odysseus a plant called moly to put into any food that Circe might offer. This protected him from her magic.

To the Underworld

Circe told Odysseus to visit the Underworld and ask the dead prophet Tiresias how to find his way home. Odysseus was dismayed, for no one ever returned from the Underworld, the home of spirits. Nevertheless, he did as Circe instructed. In the Underworld, Tiresias warned Odysseus that he'd made an enemy of Poseidon. He told Odysseus that his crew might still get home safely, as long as they didn't harm the cattle on the Sun God's island. Many other spirits came up to speak to Odysseus, including his mother and his old comrade, the warrior Achilles. Odysseus also saw Sisyphus, who spent his days trying in vain to roll a boulder up a mountain as punishment by the gods for his sins. So many wailing spirits crowded around Odysseus that he hurried back to his ship in fear.

Odysseus's mother

Odysseus saw his mother's spirit in the Underworld. He didn't even know that she had died and, overcome by grief, he tried to embrace her. She warned him that, in his absence, his family faced troubles back at home on Ithaca.

Ask the storyteller

What were Circe's instructions?

Once in the Underworld, Odysseus had to dig a pit and fill it with the blood of a specially sacrificed ram and sheep. Only when the spirits had drunk from the pit would he be able to speak to them.

Beware Sirens!

Circe was overjoyed when Odysseus returned safely from the Underworld. She wanted to help him, so she gave him instructions on how to avoid the perils that lay ahead. The men soon reached the first of these— the island of the Sirens. The Sirens were part woman, part bird. Their enchanted singing lured all who heard it to their doom on the rocks. Following Circe's advice, Odysseus filled his men's ears with wax so that they wouldn't hear the beautiful songs. Then he ordered his men to bind him tightly to the ship's mast so that he could hear the Sirens and yet survive. As they rowed near the island, Odysseus was so spellbound by the singing that he begged his men to release him. Unable to hear his pleas, the men rowed on as fast as they could and avoided disaster.

Circe's warning

Circe warned Odysseus of the dangers he and his men would find on their way home. After they had passed the Sirens, they would come to the man-eating monster, Scylla, and Charybdis, a whirlpool that sucked down ships. Circe urged Odysseus to steer a course near Scylla's cave, or Charybdis would almost certainly swallow up his crew.

What happened to the Sirens?
Some legends tell that the Sirens
hurled themselves off the rocks to
their death. They were upset
that Odysseus had heard their
song and lived to warn others
about it.

Scylla and Charybdis

Odysseus and his crew arrived at a narrow channel between steep cliffs. On one side lurked the treacherous Charybdis. On the other was the six-headed monster Scylla. Remembering Circe's advice, Odysseus told his terrified men to avoid Charybdis by sailing close to Scylla's cave. Then Odysseus armed himself and prepared to fight Scylla. The creature was too quick for him, though. Her six heads darted in all directions, snatching six of Odysseus's men in her sharp teeth.

When the ship reached the other end of the channel, the men were dazed and exhausted. They decided to rest on the Sun God's island. Odysseus warned the men not to harm the cattle, but they disobeyed. Zeus, the king of the gods, was furious. Once they'd gone to sea again, he hurled a thunderbolt at the ship. All the men drowned, except Odysseus.

The cattle of the Sun God

Odysseus had not wanted to land on the Sun God's island, but his men were exhausted and begged to rest. They promised not to harm the cattle, but when their food ran out, they secretly killed and ate two of the animals. Odysseus remembered Tiresias's warning and was horrified.

Ask the storyteller

Why did Zeus spare Odysseus?
The Sun God asked Zeus to punish the men for killing his cattle. Odysseus was spared because he was the only one who had not eaten any of the meat.

Calypso and Nausicaa

Odysseus was washed up on the island of the nymph Calypso. All his crew had died, and he was very unhappy. Although he was glad to rest at Calypso's home for a few days, she wanted to keep Odysseus with her forever and wouldn't help him leave. Feeling sorry for the hero, the gods sent their messenger, Hermes, to the island. After much persuasion, Calypso sadly agreed to let Odysseus go. She helped him make a raft, and he soon set sail once again. Poseidon was furious when he saw this and smashed the raft to pieces. For days, Odysseus was tossed in stormy seas before reaching the land of the Phaeacians. Here Princess Nausicaa found him and took him to her father's palace. When Odysseus told the Phaeacians his tragic story, they gave him one of their ships, filled with gifts, and wished him a safe journey home.

Poseidon's rage

Poseidon was still angry with Odysseus for blinding his son, the cyclops Polyphemus. He also was furious with the other gods for helping Odysseus and was determined to stop him from getting home.

Home at Last!

Odysseus awoke on yet another beach, not knowing where he was. The Phaeacians' ship had gone, and the land was shrouded in mist. Then the mist cleared, revealing the goddess Athena. When she told the hero that he was in Ithaca, Odysseus kissed the ground, overjoyed to be home at last. However, Athena had brought the hero bad news, too. She warned him that his life was in danger and told him to seek shelter at the home of his trusty swineherd, Eumaeus. Odysseus could stay there until he'd worked out a plan to destroy the enemies who now threatened him. Athena used magic to disguise the hero as an old beggar so that no one would recognize him. Gray-haired and leaning on a staff, Odysseus made his way to Eumaeus's hut. Eumaeus did not recognize his old master but greeted the beggar kindly, offering him food and shelter.

Odysseus at Eumaeus's hut

When Odysseus arrived at the hut, Eumaeus's dogs bounded out. Eumaeus had to stop them from attacking the old beggar. Odysseus lied about who he was but told the doubting Eumaeus that Odysseus was alive and would soon be home.

Why did Athena send Odysseus to stay with Eumaeus?

Athena wanted to help Odysseus, and she knew that Eumaeus was one of the few people Odysseus could trust.

The Suitors of Penelope

In the 20 years that Odysseus had been away, things had not run smoothly on Ithaca. Most people believed he would never return. For many years, Odysseus's beautiful wife, Penelope, had been plagued by dozens of men eager to marry her and rule the kingdom in Odysseus's place. Penelope still loved Odysseus and didn't want to marry any of these men, but they refused to leave her alone. They hung about the palace, gorging themselves on Odysseus's food and wine. They were also plotting to kill Odysseus's son and heir, Telemachus. Telemachus knew his life was in danger, and when Athena instructed him to go to Eumaeus's hut, he set off at once. There he was reunited with his long-lost father. Together, they worked out a plan to get rid of their enemies.

Penelope's plan

Penelope told the men that she couldn't marry anyone until she'd woven a shroud for Odysseus's father, Laertes, who was thought to be dead. However, each night she secretly undid that day's work to delay her marriage. A servant betrayed her, though, and the men demanded that she marry one of them immediately.

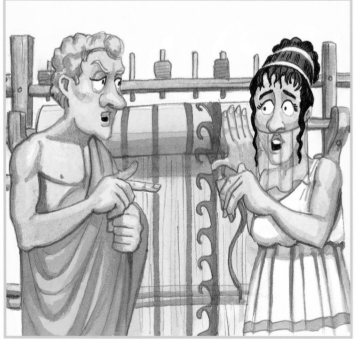

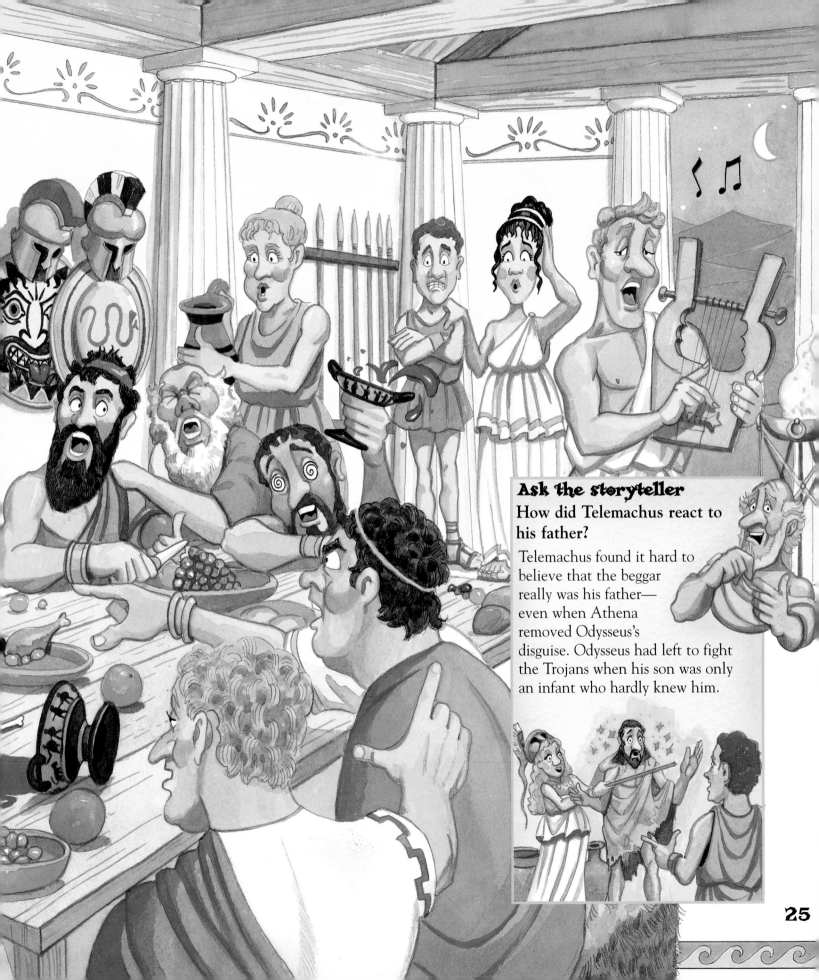

How did Telemachus react to his father?

Telemachus found it hard to believe that the beggar really was his father—even when Athena removed Odysseus's disguise. Odysseus had left to fight the Trojans when his son was only an infant who hardly knew him.

Jealous Rivals

The next morning, Odysseus traveled to the palace. He was still disguised as a beggar, and only his old dog recognized him. The men jeered when they saw the elderly man, and one of them threw a footstool at him. Odysseus was angry but knew that it was not yet the time for revenge. Irus, the brawny palace beggar, was not pleased to see someone else begging there. He challenged Odysseus to a boxing match. Odysseus agreed and astounded everyone by sending Irus sprawling with a single, well-timed blow. That night, when the men had gone home, Odysseus and Telemachus hid all the weapons the men had left at the palace. Odysseus knew that he and his son would be outnumbered in the fight, and he would need all his strength and cunning to win. He was still trying to keep his true identity secret, but was recognized by his old nurse Eurycleia.

Ask the storyteller

How did Eurycleia recognize Odysseus?

While washing Odysseus's feet, Eurycleia saw a scar on his leg. It looked just like the one that Odysseus had gotten boar-hunting as a boy. Odysseus told Eurycleia to keep his secret until he could get rid of his enemies.

Just an old beggar

When Penelope met the old beggar, she did not realize that he was her husband, Odysseus. She confessed to him that she could no longer wait for her husband to return and must agree to marry another.

A Good Shot!

The next morning, Penelope arranged an archery contest and said that she would marry the winner. The men were delighted, but none of them could even string the great bow that had belonged to Odysseus. They agreed to let the new beggar try, and to their horror, he won the contest easily. Then, disguised as a swallow, Athena led Odysseus, his son, and Eumaeus on to kill all their enemies in a bloody fight. Odysseus revealed his true identity to Penelope and his father Laertes, whom he found working in the fields nearby. The families of the dead were furious with Odysseus and marched to the palace, seeking revenge. Finding the place in an uproar, the goddess Athena persuaded everyone to end their fighting and live together peacefully again.

Odysseus and his bow

Penelope asked the men to use Odysseus's bow for the contest to test their prowess. To their amazement, the disguised Odysseus bent the great bow easily. He won the contest by sending an arrow that pierced 12 ax heads that were lined up in a row.

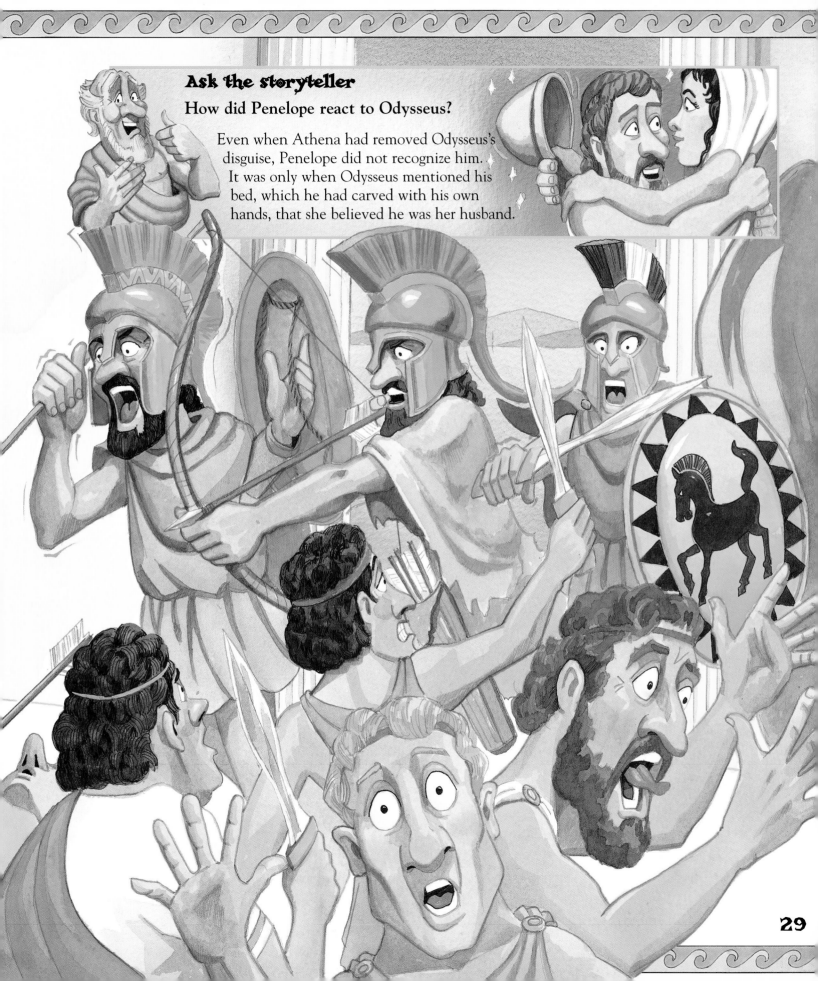

Ask the storyteller

How did Penelope react to Odysseus?

Even when Athena had removed Odysseus's disguise, Penelope did not recognize him. It was only when Odysseus mentioned his bed, which he had carved with his own hands, that she believed he was her husband.

Glossary

Channel A narrow stretch of water between two landmasses.

Cyclopes Cave-dwelling giants who had only one eye.

Heir A person who will gain the possessions and titles of someone when that person dies.

Lotus A plant with fruit that made people dreamy and forgetful.

Moly A magical herb with a black root and white flower.

Nymph A beautiful young woman related to the gods.

Prophet A person who is able to tell what will happen in the future.

Prowess Skill or strength.

Sacrifice To kill an animal and offer it to the gods.

Shroud A sheet in which a dead body is wrapped.

Sirens Creatures who were part woman, part bird, who wrecked ships by enchanting sailors onto cliffs with their songs.

Sorceress A female magician who uses magic to bewitch people.

Suitor A man who is seeking a woman's hand in marriage.

Swineherd A person who looks after pigs.

Trojan War A war between the Greeks and the city of Troy because a Trojan prince stole the wife of a Greek king.

Underworld The place in Greek mythology where people go after they die.

Who's Who

Achilles (uh-KILL-eez) A Greek warrior who fought in the Trojan War.

Aeolus (EE-uh-luss) The god who controlled the winds.

Antiphates (an-TIFF-at-eez) The king of the Laestrygonians.

Athena (uh-THEE-na) Zeus's daughter and the Greek goddess of wisdom and war.

Calypso (ka-LIP-so) An island nymph.

Charybdis (ka-RIB-diss) A monster that lived in a whirlpool and sucked down passing ships.

Cicones (si-KOH-neez) A tribe who lived near Ismarus.

Circe (SIR-see) A sorceress who turned men into animals.

Eumaeus (you-MAY-us) The swineherd who sheltered Odysseus on his return to Ithaca.

Eurycleia (yoo-ree-CLAY-ah) Odysseus's nurse who cared for him when he was a boy.

Hermes (HER-meez) The messenger of the gods, who wore winged sandals to carry him over land and sea.

Laestrygonians (lice-tree-GO-nee-ans) A race of man-eating giants.

Nausicaa (naw-SICK-ay-ah) A Phaeacian princess whose father helped Odysseus get home.

Odysseus (oh-DISS-ee-us) A Greek hero.

Penelope (puh-NELL-uh-pee) The wife of Odysseus.

Phaeacians (fee-AY-shunz) A race of people who helped Odysseus get home.

Polyphemus (poll-ee-FEE-muss) A cyclops.

Poseidon (poss-EYE-don) The Greek god of the sea.

Scylla (SILL-uh) A six-headed, man-eating monster that lived in a cave.

Sisyphus (SISS-if-us) A man who had to spend his time in the Underworld trying to roll a boulder up a mountain.

Telemachus (te-LEM-ah-kuss) The son and heir of Odysseus.

Tiresias (tie-REE-see-as) The dead prophet of the Underworld.

Zeus (ZOOS) King of the Greek gods.

Index